Thoughts *from* Walden Pond

by Henry David Thoreau

Photographs by Charles Gurche • Text by Dona Budd

Pomegranate

SAN FRANCISCO

To Sara Ashley Devins,
who sees and lives with passion.

• CG

For my sisters Beth and Z. Katie,
who like it when I write.

• DB

Published by Pomegranate
Box 6099, Rohnert Park, CA 94927

Pomegranate Europe Ltd.
Fullbridge House, Fullbridge
Maldon, Essex CM9 4LE, England

Photographs © 1998 Charles Gurche
Text © 1998 Dona Budd

Cover and interior design
by Crowfoot Design Group

Printed in Hong Kong
07 06 05 04 03 02 01 00 99 98
10 9 8 7 6 5 4 3 2 1

Pomegranate Catalog No. A921
ISBN 0-7649-0617-8

Library of Congress Cataloging-in-Publication Data

Gurche, Charles.
    Thoughts from Walden Pond by Henry David
Thoreau / photographs by Charles Gurche : text by
Dona Budd.
       p.   cm.
    Includes bibliographical references.
    "Selected works by Henry David Thoreau": p.
    ISBN 0-7649-0617-8 (pbk. : alk. paper)
    1. Thoreau, Henry David, 1817–1862—
Quotations. 2. Thoreau, Henry David, 1817–1862—
Homes and haunts—Massachusetts—Walden Woods
—Pictorial works. 3. Walden Woods (Mass.)—
Pictorial works. 4. Quotations, American.
I. Thoreau, Henry David, 1817–1862. II. Budd, Dona.
III. Title.
PS3048.A3   1998   97-44955
818 '.309—dc21   CIP

C O N T E N T S

ENRY DAVID THOREAU'S *WALDEN*, written in 1854—the occasion for this collection of photographs—focuses on a very specific period in the author's life: the two years, two months, and two days he spent living in a cabin he built less than a hundred feet from the northern bay of Walden Pond, about a mile and a half south of the village of Concord, Massachusetts. He moved in on July 4, 1845, eight days before his twenty-eighth birthday, and left on September 6, 1847, a few weeks after his thirtieth birthday.

The written account condenses that two-year period into one complete cycle of seasons, producing a neater and more economical literary form. Thoreau's close physical and spiritual relationship to Walden Pond and the surrounding woods, however, lasted a lifetime.

One of Thoreau's first memories, in fact, was of a visit he made to Walden Pond when he was four years old. He and his family had returned to Concord from Boston, where they had lived for a short time, to call on his maternal grandmother on the farm where Thoreau had been born. In the journal he began when he left Harvard University, Thoreau recorded that trip to the pond as

one of the most ancient scenes stamped on the tablets of my memory. . . . That sweet solitude my spirit seemed so early to require at once gave the preference to this recess among the pines, where almost sunshine and shadow were the only inhabitants that varied the scene, over that tumultuous and varied city, as if it had found its proper nursery.[1]

Thoreau visited Walden Pond for the last time, accompanied by his sister Sophia, in late September 1861. He was very ill, in his final bout with tuberculosis, and died less than eight months later, several weeks before his forty-fourth birthday. On this last visit to the pond, having gathered some of the grapes that grew wild in the nearby woods, he dropped them one at a time into the water—noting, I'll bet, with his remarkable powers of observation, some last phenomenon of plop, minnow scatter, ripple, displacement, and sink.

Between those two visits, this writer, poet, philosopher, naturalist, pencil manufacturer, and village oddball lived mostly with his parents and three siblings (two sisters and an adored brother) in Concord, population about two thousand. None of the four ever married. Thoreau walked to Walden Pond frequently, seeing it, he wrote, "almost daily for more than twenty years." [2] When he was seven, he helped boil chowder on a sandbar that ran out into the water. In his youth, he would row his boat to the middle of the pond and lie on his back, "dreaming awake," [3] drifting until startled by the boat striking shore. At the end of one nighttime fishing trip, Thoreau and a companion created a light show by flinging glowing brands from their beach fire into the water.

During the period when he lived in the woods, Thoreau wrote *A Week on the Concord and Merrimack Rivers* (1849)—his first published book—and an early version of Walden. When *Week* came out, however, it was a commercial flop, and publication of *Walden* was delayed until 1854, seven years after Thoreau left his cabin by the pond. He continued to expand and revise the book considerably, incorporating experiences and observations from the intervening years. It's a complicated matter, then, not only to establish which period of Thoreau's life the book refers to but also to determine when it was actually written.

For instance, Thoreau tells us the dates of the freezings and thawings of Walden Pond for most years, right up to the spring of the publication year. At one point, in describing the thundering of a thawing pond, he writes: "Who would have suspected so large and cold and thick-skinned a thing to be so sensitive? The earth is all alive and covered with papilae." [4] Here, however, he refers specifically to the thundering of another local pond, Flints' Pond, in February 1850, three years after he moved back to town. Thoreau's two years in the woods, then, were finally not so much the subject of the book as the foundation of a continuing reflection on and enlarging of the experience. *Walden* offers a version of that period of retreat, layered through years of living and contemplation.

Just as Thoreau's experience of Walden Pond, as well as the book it inspired, extends outward in time, his retreat into the wild extended out into civilization, and civilization visited his forest habitation. In fact, when *Walden* was finally published, book reviewers for various journals were annoyed with Thoreau for representing himself as living apart from civilization while making frequent trips to Concord, where he often took dinner with friends. If he has spurned civilization, they wondered, why is he dining so often off Ralph Waldo Emerson's china? And living near the Fitchburg Railroad, which skirts one shore of the pond, and receiving visits not only from vagrants and various passersby but also from respectable acquaintances and literary figures? It didn't sound so terribly wild.

Perhaps a reply is indicated in Thoreau's description of church bells heard through an expanse of woods:

> Sometimes, on Sundays, I heard the bells . . . when the wind was favorable, a faint, sweet, and, as it were, natural melody, worth importing into the wilderness. At a sufficient distance over the woods this sound acquires a certain vibratory hum, as if the pine needles in the horizon were the strings of a harp which it swept. All sound heard at the greatest possible distance produces one and the same effect, a vibration of the universal lyre. . . . There came to me in this case a melody which the air had strained, and which had conversed with every leaf and needle of the wood, that portion of the sound which the elements had taken up and modulated and echoed from vale to vale. The echo is, to some extent, an original sound, and therein is the magic and charm of it. It is not merely a repetition of what was worth repeating in the bell, but partly the voice of the wood.[5]

The wood is a medium that sifts the sound. There is a magic and charm (charm in the sense of bewitching as well as appealing) about the wood that transforms the strains of civilization that arrive from a distance. The distance itself is modulating, and the wood, the elements, the landscape are purifying. By analogy, we can imagine that the railroad, the visitors, the dinners blew through the intervening woods to Walden Pond. We can imagine likewise that the two years at Walden Pond blew into the book through the following seven years.

It is a mistake, then, to think of the Walden experience as two years crammed into a one-year literary package. That view fails to make clear the extent to which the content of *Walden* represents a lifetime of association with the pond and woods, as well as the lifetime of intellectual and spiritual work the pond and woods fostered as the "proper nursery" of Thoreau's spirit. It is illuminating to recognize and think about the larger context of *Walden*. When I notice the ways in which *Walden* extends outward in time and spirit, into Thoreau's life and beyond, it makes my engagement with the book richer, and more fun. And if Thoreau was doing anything, he was having fun, in spite of his plain diet and reputed celibacy.

This tendency of the book to "get up and move around," out of its time frame and into Thoreau's life and, finally, even further—away from the nineteenth century and away from Thoreau—harmonizes surprisingly with the practice of picturing *Walden*. Creating visual images from *Walden* constitutes an effort to cross time boundaries, to import into the present moment the qualities of the book and the life. It also reflects the processes of mind and spirit, and even the physical organization, of the man who created *Walden* in the first place, a man with a stunning capacity to *see*. The quality of Thoreau's power of observation, and his passion for observing, shaped his spiritual, intellectual, and quotidian life.

A BIOGRAPHICAL SKETCH

In 1817, the year of Thoreau's birth, Concord was a small town rooted in a farm economy. It also profited, both financially and socially, from being on the main route from Boston to other towns in New England. Concord's citizens were primarily white Protestants of English and Scottish origin, though Thoreau also had French ancestors. The name apparently has turned up in medieval documents from Tours, France.

Thoreau's family background reveals people of gumption and integrity. During the American Revolution, when his great-uncles were jailed for being Tories, Thoreau's maternal grandmother hid files in food she brought to them (is she to blame for the device used in all those cowboy and prison movies?) and stole horses for their escape. His paternal grandfather survived a shipwreck, arriving in Boston penniless. He eventually established a prosperous store, starting out with nothing but sixty-three gallons of sugar. Thoreau's maternal grandfather became the hero of his Harvard class by leading a successful uprising against the university's administration, demanding better food.

Thoreau's father, John, apparently was amiable and easygoing and loved music and books. He moved his young family from Concord to smaller Chelmsford, ten miles away, and then to Boston, trying without success to make a go of it as a storekeeper. The family moved back to Concord in 1823 when John went into the pencil-making business with his otherwise unreliable brother-in-law, who had found a mine of high-quality graphite. The firm put the family on its feet financially at last, providing a modest but steady income. When Henry returned home from Harvard, he experimented with graphite mixtures to develop the only pencils in America that rivaled the quality of those made in England. When his father died in 1859, he took on the main responsibility for running the business.

His mother, born Cynthia Dunbar, was energetic, community minded, generous, outspoken, and nobody's fool; ran an orderly household with a certain grace; and cofounded the Concord Women's Anti-Slavery Society. Following her lead, Henry became a conductor on the Underground Railroad, assisting runaway slaves on their journey to freedom in Canada. Cynthia passed on her love of nature to her children, taking them on excursions into the woods and schooling them in observation of the natural world. She sometimes cooked their dinner outdoors over an open fire. She must have been the leading spirit of the family and

a model of vigor, self-confidence, and strong-mindedness for her son. Henry was third of the four children. His sister Helen, who taught school and gave lessons in music and painting, was born five months after her parents' marriage. She died before Henry did, of tuberculosis, the same disease that ended his life. Sophia, the youngest, was much like her mother, it seems: energetic, capable, and confident. She also taught school, and she loved music and flowers. After Henry's death, she took over the family pencil business, in spite of contrary assumptions about what was appropriate for women to do.

Henry had a particularly strong tie with the second-born, his brother, John. People in the community saw John as more amiable and gregarious than the solemn and peculiar Henry, and they liked him better, a difference that did not seem to damage the brothers' bond. John contributed to Henry's college expenses when it was decided to send Henry rather than John to Harvard, though some townspeople saw John as the genius of the family. After Harvard, the brothers taught together at Concord Academy, which Henry founded when the village school folded. They introduced innovations such as the abolishment of corporal punishment, though they kept strict discipline, and field trips during which students learned local and natural history, practiced surveying, and, at Concord's *Yoeman's Gazette*, watched the setting of type. Henry proposed marriage only once, to a woman with whom both he and John had fallen in love. She had refused John before she refused him.

A Week on the Concord and Merrimack Rivers is based on a boating trip the two brothers took in 1839. Henry wrote it as a tribute to John, who died in his brother's arms in 1842, at the age of twenty-six. He had contracted lockjaw after cutting his finger slightly in stropping his razor. Eleven days after John's death, Henry developed severe sympathetic symptoms, and the horrified family prepared to lose a second member to lockjaw. His recovery took months, and he was gripped by depression for much longer. He could not bring himself to sing, formerly one of his chief pleasures.

There seems to have existed between the brothers a kind of twinness, suggested by their choice to work and play together and by Henry's incorporation of symptoms of his brother's illness.

The local minister's eulogy for John shows that others noticed their similarities:

> There is not a hill, nor a tree, nor a bird, nor a flower of marked beauty in all this neighbor-hood that he was not familiar with, and any new bird or flower he discovered gave the most unfeigned delight, and he would commune with it for hours. . . . He had a heart to feel and a voice to speak for all classes of suffering humanity; and the cause of the poor inebriate, the slave, the ignorant and depraved, was very dear to him. . . . [H]is principles and religious feeling were always unshaken.[6]

Exhibiting the same qualities, Henry was always more interested in the poor, the misfit, and the distressed than in the more conventional and comfortable Concordians. Reflecting John's intimacy with nature, Henry claimed he could tell the month by the plants that were in bloom. In later years, the community recognized him as an expert naturalist and neighbors brought him specimens to identify.

It is tempting to ponder what role this fraternal bond and identification might have played in shaping Thoreau's genius and leading him to write *Walden*. I find myself imagining that the daunting assurance and authority with which Thoreau speaks in *Walden* is connected to his being the accepted comrade of a worshiped elder brother who held the same ideals and enthusiasms. This imagined benefit may spring from my own envy.

Thoreau recorded a number of childhood memories in his journal. He was kicked by an ox; he tried to smoke the dried stems of the water lily; and he and his brother caught an eel. His publisher relates that in his boyhood, Thoreau had a favorite cow among those he drove to pasture, and years later he spoke of her with as much tenderness as if "she had been his own grandmother."[7]

As a young boy, Thoreau feared thunderstorms and didn't want to go to heaven because he feared he wouldn't be able to take his sled. He revealed his spiritual sensibility early on when he told his mother, who had found him lying awake late in his trundle bed, "I have been looking through the stars to see if I could see God behind them." Thoreau was never willing, however, to identify with any religious denomination, and his strong spiritual life remained individualistic. It needed to include sleds.

Thoreau's schoolmates, not surprisingly, recognized his difference without recognizing its quality. Rather than joining in their games, he preferred to observe quietly, and they found him strange and too serious. They nicknamed him "Judge" and teased him as "the fine scholar with the big nose." As it turned out, Thoreau later became dissatisfied with scholarship, finding it too far removed from practical experience and the truth of the practical and the natural world, where his inspirations and insights were anchored. Commenting on his Harvard education, he writes in *Walden*: "To my astonishment I was informed on leaving college that I had studied navigation! —why, if I had taken one turn down the harbor I should have known more about it."[8]

Thoreau was also given nicknames as an adult—the "Concord Pan" and "Philosophic Woodchuck." He spent hours walking in the woods most days of his life, and his rejection of conventional ideas and behavior inevitably drew censure from the small-town adult world as well as his peers in the schoolyard. It's hard to guess which might have been more distasteful to local industrious citizens busy at establishing their fortunes and families—Thoreau's contempt for their pursuit of prosperity or his devotion to living on his own terms so that he could "front only the essential facts of life, and see if I could not learn what it had to teach, and not, when I came to die, discover that I had not lived."[9] To neighbors, his way of living—making regular visits to favorite trees, spending an entire day listening to a pond—looked like goofing off, squandering the Harvard education his parents, siblings, and aunts had pooled their talents and moderate resources to provide.

A farmer reported finding Thoreau standing in the same spot observing a muddy pond when he passed by three times in one day, morning, noon, and evening. The man reported their early evening exchange, initiated by the farmer:

> "[W]hat air you a-doin'?" And he didn't turn his head and he didn't look at me. He kept on lookin' down at that pond, and he said, as if he was thinkin' about the stars in the heavens, "Mr. Murray, I'm a-studyin'—the habits—of the bullfrog!" And there that darned fool had been standin'—the livelong day—a-studyin'—the habits—of the *bull*-frog![10]

Even fellow literary lions who admired Thoreau sometimes found him hard to bear. Nathaniel Hawthorne once described Thoreau as "the most unmalleable fellow alive—the most tedious, tiresome, and intolerable—the narrowest

and most notional—and yet, true as all this is, he has great qualities of intellect and character."[11]

It would be an exaggeration to say, however, that Thoreau was alienated from the community. As time went by, his knowledge of nature was increasingly respected and consulted, and he received from local people gifts of natural objects —birds' nests, unusual rocks, feathers, and so forth. (During the last years of his life, he made the attic of the family house into his own room, something between a monk's cell and a boy's own corner, with his simple Walden Pond cot for a bed and his collection of natural objects resting on the shelves he had built around the room.) As a young man, he participated with his brother in the social events arranged for Concord youth and began giving annual melon parties. Everyone was eager to attend these parties in order to enjoy the especially delicious, sometimes even exotic, melons Thoreau put special effort into growing.

Thoreau did have enthusiastic admirers, particularly among the writers, intellectuals, and others who were attracted to the intellectual buzz around his neighbor Ralph Waldo

Emerson. Some who were initially drawn to Emerson wound up neglecting him in their fascination with the younger, less tamed and more vivid, if less socially charming, man.

Emerson had moved to Concord by 1834, and in 1836 he published *Nature*, a book that placed him at the focal point of an intellectual stir that came to be called Transcendentalism. The more established literary figure inspired and supported young Thoreau, who was drawn to the Transcendentalist faith in the power of human spiritual insight—the power to perceive God immanent in the natural world—over Enlightenment rationality based on mechanistic observation of material facts as the legitimate way to perceive what is true. Thoreau even lived with the Emersons at times during his young adulthood, earning his keep by doing the household building, repair, and maintenance work, at which he, unlike Emerson, was impressively skilled. In later years, however, the friendship cooled as the two men's ideas diverged and they became disappointed in each other.

The record of the adult Thoreau's interaction with children shows his capacity for a generous sympathy. When, in 1849, Emerson's little girl Ellen was sent to her uncle's home on Staten Island, New York, to regain her health after a bout with mumps, Henry wrote her a letter:

I think that we are pretty well acquainted, though we never had any very long talks. We have had a good many short talks, at any rate. . . . Don't you remember our wise criticisms on the pictures in the portfolio and the Turkish book with Eddy and Edith looking on,—how almost any pictures answered our purpose, and we went through the Penny Magazine, first from beginning to end, and then from end to beginning, and Eddy stared just as much the second time as the first, and Edith thought that we turned over too soon, and that there were some things which she had not seen—? I can guess pretty well what interests you, and what you think about. Indeed I am interested in pretty much the same things myself. I suppose you think that persons who are as old as your father and myself are always thinking about very grave things, but I know that we are meditating the same old themes that we did when we were ten years old, only we go more gravely about it. . . .

. . . I was present at the celebration of [Eddy's] birthday lately, and supplied the company with onion and squash pipes, and rhubarb whistles, which is the most I can do on such occasions. Little Sammy Hoar blowed them most successfully, and made the loudest noise, though it almost strained his eyes out to do it. . . .

Do not think that you must write to me because I have written to you. It does not follow at all. . . . Yet if sometime it should be perfectly easy, and pleasant to you, I shall be very glad to have a sentence.[12]

Thoreau had spent six months as a tutor in the same household prior to Ellen's stay—one of the few times he lived away from Concord — and had been very dissatisfied and homesick during his time there.

There are a number of accounts of Thoreau's relationship with local children. He rarely allowed adults to accompany him on his long daily walks in the woods, aside from his closest friend, William Ellery Channing, the more or less ne'er-do-well nephew of the famous divine of the same name (he was the sort of convention-flouting person Henry tended to be attracted to). He was willing to interrupt his solitude, however, for children, and sometimes several would join him on an expedition. On such occasions, Thoreau might reveal the secrets of plants or point out the habits of animals, showing the amazed group how to catch fish in their hands, for instance. On one huckleberry-gathering party he led for some youngsters, he consoled a boy who had spilled his basketful by revealing to him that in order to keep having huckleberries, nature needed boys who would sometimes spill some on the ground, and if the boy came to the same spot a full year later, he would find a lush harvest of berries.

One of the children who knew Thoreau was Louisa May Alcott. She recalled:

He gravely informed us once, that frogs were much more confiding in the spring, than later in the season; for then it only took an hour to get well acquainted with one of the speckled swimmers, who liked to be tickled with a blade of grass, and would feed from his hand in the most sociable manner.[13]

A friend of the Alcott children wrote of Thoreau taking the group out on Walden Pond and

ceasing his oars after a little distance from the shore and playing the flute he had brought with him. . . . He suddenly laid the flute down and told us stories of the Indians that "long ago" had lived about Walden and Concord; delighting us with simple, clear explanations of the wonders of Walden woods.[14]

Another child, however, recorded later in his life his view of "this strange man" when the boy was sent to carry a message to Thoreau's mother. His account shows what he had picked up of local gossip, referring to an occasion, long resented in the community, when Thoreau and a friend had accidentally burned a stand of woods, and to Thoreau's stash of about seven hundred unsold copies of the thousand-copy first printing of *A Week on the Concord and Merrimack Rivers:*

> He stood in the doorway with hair which looked as if it had been dressed with a pine-cone, inattentive grey eyes, hazy with far-away musings, an emphatic nose and disheveled attire that bore signs of tramps in woods and swamps. Thinking of the forest fire I fancied he smelled of smoke and peered curiously up the staircase behind him hoping I might get a glimpse of that queer library all of one book duplicated one thousand times.[15]

Thoreau's private life and public literary career intersect in his journal, the written record of his experiences and thoughts that became the foundation of his public work. In an important sense, he launched his literary career on October 22, 1837, the day of the first journal entry. His work actually moved into the public arena, however, on April 11, 1838, when he gave his first lecture at the Concord Lyceum.

In the mid-1820s, Josiah Holbrook initiated the lyceum movement in Massachusetts with the intention of bringing knowledge and intellectual stimulation to local communities by establishing a series of lectures and debates. Thoreau may have begun attending these events as a boy, considering his intellectual and literary interests, and those of his parents, when the Concord Lyceum was established in 1829. All community members, including children, were welcome. There must be some connection between the lyceums and the section in *Walden* in which Thoreau expresses disappointment with his Harvard education and offers the notion that villages should be universities. After Thoreau gave his first lecture at the Concord Lyceum, six months after he began his journal, he spoke there regularly for the rest of his life. Lecturing was, for one thing, a way to make money, and subsequently he gave talks in other towns as well. Lecturing also provided Thoreau with a platform, and honoring learning, inquiry, and debate as the lyceums did, it must have helped endow him with a certain value in the public eye in spite of his idiosyncrasy and sometimes prickly individuality.

Thoreau's first journal entry, made when he was twenty, reads: "'What are you doing now?' he asked. 'Do you keep a journal?' So I make my first entry today."[16] We don't know who asked this question; maybe Emerson. But it launched the daily writings from which Thoreau largely drew his lectures, essays, and books. The journal writing is the seed, and often the substance, of his literary production.

Thoreau's last journal entry, made when he was very ill and nearing the period when he was unable even to read, records his recognizing the slant of a heavy rainfall by the pattern of some scattered gravel. He concludes: "All this is perfectly distinct to an observant eye, and yet could easily pass unnoticed by most."[17]

Thoreau associated with most of the leading literary figures of the day—Nathaniel Hawthorne, Margaret Fuller, and Walt Whitman, as well as Emerson and others. No doubt the intellectual climate he lived in nourished him in important ways, but you never get the sense that he had anyone else's light in his eye. Intellectually, as in all other ways, he unerringly practiced what he preached:

> Let every one mind his own business, and endeavor to be what he was made. . . . If a man does not keep pace with his companions, perhaps it is because he hears a different drummer. Let him step to the music which he hears, however measured or far away.[18]

Thoreau never danced to any band but his own.

Perhaps predictably, he did not receive much public acclaim in his lifetime, a circumstance foreshadowed by the early fate of *A Week on the Concord and Merrimack Rivers*. After he had stacked up in his house the more than seven hundred copies the publisher couldn't sell or give away, he wryly commented in his journal that he now had a library numbering over nine hundred volumes, more than seven hundred of which he himself had written.[19]

Walden was the last of Thoreau's books to be published during his life. Had *Week* been successful, however, and *Walden* published on schedule, it would have lacked the enrichment of the subsequent revisions and additions. In the second paragraph of the final work, Thoreau refers to the circumstances of its inception. He writes, "I should not obtrude my affairs so much on the notice of my readers if very particular inquiries had not been made by my townsmen concerning my mode of life." His townspeople truly were curious about his life in the woods; in fact, Walden began as a series of lyceum lectures responding to their curiosity.

The reviews of *Walden* that appeared when it was first published are mixed, and often of a certain recognizable mixture. Fairly typical is this comment from the abolitionist journal *National*

Era: "With all its extravagances, its sophisms, and its intellectual pride, the book is acute and suggestive, and contains passages of great beauty." The same issues come up over and over. More negative reviews object to a scolding tone, radical social criticism, and affronts to religious orthodoxy but grudgingly acknowledge passages of wisdom and beauty. More positive reviews praise the book's beauty and courage, its many pearls of wisdom, and Thoreau's knowledge and descriptions of nature and apologize for his unorthodox religious views and high-handed preachiness. It is striking how this double response to the book —admiration on one hand and irritation on the other—reflects the character of the world's response to the man. In both cases, there is a neither-here-nor-thereness that suggests you can never merely sum up the book or the man. All you can do is look at what is right in front of you at the moment and watch it transform all the time.

"Civil Disobedience" may be Thoreau's best-known essay. Typically, it arose from a notable personal experience. In 1846, Thoreau was jailed overnight for refusing to pay his poll tax (a fixed tax levied on all adults). He was following the example of other abolitionists who would not support in this form a government that tolerated slavery. He was furious when the next day his aunt paid the tax for him, and he had to be threatened with being thrown out before he would leave jail. Following the incident, he gave a lyceum lecture to explain his position to his townsfolk. Published in 1849 in *Aesthetic Papers*, the lecture became his most influential political essay. Thoreau's other books were published after his death, including *The Maine Woods* and *Cape Cod*, based, like *Walden*, on his experiences of particular landscapes.

Thoreau's literary career was hardly remunerative, and the combination of odd jobs and spare economy he practiced at Walden Pond corresponds to the way he lived most of his life. He worked willingly with his hands, being a skilled carpenter and handyman. He also became an expert land surveyor. Lecturing brought some income, but opportunities didn't come his way as often as he would have liked. He discusses making a living in *Walden*, where he writes that teaching and trade took him out of his way and he'd had "some sad experience in conforming to the wishes of friends." He also contemplates gathering huckleberries, wild herbs, and evergreens to market in town but decides that "though you trade in messages from heaven, the whole curse of trade attaches to the business." After considering these alternatives, he concludes:

> As I preferred some things to others, and especially valued my freedom, as I could fare hard and yet succeed well, I did not wish to spend my time in earning rich carpets or other fine furniture, or delicate cookery, or a house in the Grecian or the Gothic style just yet. If there are any to whom it is no interruption to acquire these things, and who know how to use them when acquired, I relinquish to them the pursuit.[20]

The core of Thoreau's genius, for me, is his ability to remain persistently conscious of his true direction. He remembered, remarkably, that he preferred some things to others and would not accept interruption. In his letter to little Ellen Emerson during her convalescence from mumps, he predicts that she will follow his example:

> You love to write or to read a fairy story and that is what you will always like to do, in some form or other. By and by you will discover that you want what are called the necessaries of life only that you may realize some such dream.[21]

In *Walden*, Thoreau champions and celebrates what he prefers to do and the philosophy that lets him do it. It strikes me that this comes off the page in two ways. One way appears to insist that his way of life is the most worthy, practical, and wise and only fools would live differently. The other way gives the impression that he advocates the pursuit of freedom only and that to dictate or accept rules, even from Henry Thoreau, is wrongheaded and bad. My guess is that he believed both.

Thoreau had a remarkable death, as indicated by the record friends and family left of his slow dying. It would be hard to say when he first began to suffer from the tuberculosis that killed his sister Helen and his paternal grandfather. It may have troubled him to some degree throughout his adult life. But over several months, in 1860 and 1861, he became gradually weaker. By November of the latter year, he was wasted and clearly dying—as a friend of the family wrote,

> "A flush had come to his cheeks and an ominous brightness and beauty to his eyes, painful to behold.His conversation was unusually brilliant, and we listened with charmed attention."[22]

In December, his sister Sophia wrote, "His spirits do not fail him, he continues in his usual serene mood, which is very pleasant for his friends as well as himself."[23] In January 1862, a friend who ice-skated down the Concord River to visit found him pretty low, but well enough to be up in his chair. . . . There was a beautiful snowstorm going on the while which I fancy inspired him, and his talk was up to the best I ever heard from him,—the same depth of earnestness and the same infinite depth of fun going on at the same time. . . . He seemed to be in an exalted state of mind for a long time before his death. He said it was just as good to be sick as to be well,—just as good to have a poor time as a good time.[24]

In March, in dictating to his sister a grateful reply to a young poet who had praised his work, Thoreau said, "I *suppose* that I have not many months to live; but, of course, I know nothing about it. I may add that I am enjoying existence as much as ever, and regret nothing."[25]

In April, Sophia wrote,

"For many weeks he has spoken only in a faint whisper. Henry accepts this dispensation with such childlike trust and is so happy that I feel as if he were being translated rather than dying in the ordinary way."[26]

Emerson recorded in his journal a visit to Thoreau by Sam Staples, who had jailed Thoreau for not paying his taxes. Staples said that he never "saw a man dying with so much pleasure and peace."[27]

Seeing children from his window, Thoreau asked Sophia to invite them in. They returned often afterward because they liked to. He told Sophia that there was as much comfort in perfect disease as in perfect health.[28]

Thoreau died at nine o'clock on the morning of May 6, 1862. His last discernible words were "Moose" and "Indian." His mother and sister and his aunt Louisa were watching over him. Sophia later said, "I feel as if something very beautiful had happened—not death."[29] At his funeral were some hypocrites, but more who felt truly bereft. Of Concord's four hundred school-children, three hundred followed Thoreau's coffin from the church to the grave.

THOREAU SEEING/SEEING THOREAU

I began contemplating the character of this book by asking myself, What do photographs and *Walden* have to do with each other? As I read and thought, I began to see Thoreau himself at the fulcrum of the question, so it changed a bit. Then I asked, What is there *about Thoreau* that connects photographs and *Walden*? I told myself a lot of complicated answers, but then all I had was a rattling bagful of complicated answers. Finally, one morning in the shower, I was watching water drops cling to the shower curtain and then, according to their size (that is to say, weight) and the surface tension of the drier or wetter spots of curtain, creep and finally speed down to the hem, hijacking any other droplets the original mass collided with or even skimmed by, getting blobbier and faster until my eyes couldn't keep up. And I began to bet on which of any random two drops would first plunge hellward. As I stood rapt while the hot water ran out, I found the key—well, my key—to the connection between picturing and *Walden*: seeing. It is seeing that links picturing and *Walden*.

When I first read *Walden*, it was a forced march. Like many, maybe most of us, I had *Walden* imposed on me in the unhappy circumstance of a classroom assignment and reacted allergically. Yet I have carried with me ever since the astonishing image of a prosperous farmer pushing, all his life, his barn:

> I see young men, my townsmen, whose misfortune it is to have inherited farms, houses, barns, cattle, and farming tools; for these are more easily acquired than got rid of. . . . They have got to live a man's life, pushing all these things before them, and get on as well as they can. How many a poor immortal soul have I met well nigh crushed and smothered under its load, creeping down the road of life, pushing before it a barn seventy-five feet by forty, its Augean stables never cleansed, and one hundred acres of land, tillage, mowing, pasture, and wood-lot! [30]

It was impossible for me to escape the impact of this vision—the transformation of prosperity into a brutish chore, oppressive and absurd. The picture of it is compelling in a way logic cannot be. Watching the image is like watching a freak show. It makes your muscles ache. It gets a hook into you. It makes you want to live in a hut by a lake, with squirrels under the floorboards.

Some readers of and writers about *Walden* complain that the logic of Thoreau's economics and politics doesn't hold up. They seem to know about these things and are probably right. But *Walden* is not powered by logic; it is powered by seeing. This book puts faith in a holy apprehension of ultralogical truth, a truth you glimpse only by paying extraordinary attention to what's in front of your face.

In his central statement on seeing, Thoreau insists that a certain quality and power of seeing provides the only access to any elevated or genuine art, knowledge, or experience:

> No method nor discipline can supersede the necessity of being forever on the alert. What is a course of history, or philosophy, or poetry, no matter how well selected, or the best society,

or the most admirable routine of life, compared with the discipline of looking always at what is to be seen? Will you be a reader, a student merely, or a seer?[31]

In Thoreau's use of "seer" here, the plain sense of "looker" is as present as the magical sense of perceiver of mysteries. For Thoreau the two senses of the word were virtually the same. And what demonstrates that his sweeping statement is not only metaphorical, only fancy language, are the dominance, intensity, and revelatory power of the visual images in the book itself. In one of *Walden's* many lyrical moments, Thoreau describes the appearance of the pond on a calm September day:

It is like molten glass cooled but not congealed, and the few motes in it are pure and beautiful like the imperfections in glass. . . . It is a soothing employment, on one of those fine days in the fall when all the warmth of the sun is fully appreciated, to sit on a stump on such a height as this, overlooking the pond, and study the dimpling circles which are incessantly inscribed on its otherwise invisible surface amid the reflected skies and trees. Over this great expanse there is no disturbance but it is thus at once gently smoothed away and assuaged. . . . Not a fish can leap or an insect fall on the pond but it is thus reported in circling dimples, in lines of beauty, as it were the constant welling up of its fountain, the gentle pulsing of its life, the heaving of its breast. The thrills of joy and thrills of pain are indis-

tinguishable. How peaceful the phenomena of the lake! Again the works of man shine as in the spring.[32]

He's talking about blips on a pond. But the quality of his seeing registers the complexity of line and reflection, motion and cease so that he sees the breath and blood of the pond and the regeneration of the work of humankind. It's not that seeing is believing; it's that seeing, for Thoreau, is the primary operation of the spirit.

In contrast to this distant elevated view, Thoreau gets an ultra-close-up when he stoops to drink from an opening he has chopped in the ice:

[K]neeling to drink, I look down into the quiet parlor of the fishes, pervaded by a softened light as through a window of ground glass, with its bright sanded floor the same as in summer; there a perennial waveless serenity reigns as in the amber twilight sky, corresponding to the cool and even temperament of the inhabitants. Heaven is under our feet as well as over our heads.[33]

What he peers through is not just some hole cut in the ice to scoop up a drink or jerk food out on a line. It is a window on an order of life—what's down there becomes food by accident and misfortune but is in fact a colony of beings, inhabitants. It's a parlor—of fishes. *Seeing* the parlor transforms the life of the pond. The hole in the ice is also (almost literally for Thoreau) a gate to heaven, that is, access to a holy act of seeing.

Judging by the value of seeing, Thoreau finds that Flints' Pond is misnamed:

Flints' Pond! Such is the poverty of our nomenclature. What right had the unclean and stupid farmer, whose farm abutted on this sky water, whose shores he has ruthlessly laid bare, to give his name to it? Some skin-flint, who loved better the reflecting surface of a dollar, or a bright cent, in which he could see his own brazen face. . . . [S]o it is not named for me. I go not there to see him nor to hear of him; who never *saw* it, who never bathed in it, who never loved it, who never protected it, who never spoke a good word for it, nor thanked God that he had made it.[34]

The unworthy Flints is making at least a couple of mistakes. First, he's looking at the wrong thing. Neither his own ruthless reflection nor the face of a coin has a chance of showing him the parlor of fishes or the regeneration of humankind. Second, since his face reflects the brass of the coin and the coin reflects the brass of his face, well, what's what? He's caught in brass barbers' mirrors of infinite mutual reflection, where he cannot locate the original real thing. In fact, old money-faced Flints cannot see

any real thing. And of all the things the insufficiently washed Flints never did with the pond, never *seeing* it comes first and is underscored; it's the worst. Thoreau forecloses on Flints' pond because of Flints' crime of failing to look and failing to see.

There is a striking moment in Walden when we see Thoreau seeing—when he is not simply telling us what he has observed. We catch him in the act, stretched out facedown on the ice of the pond:

The first ice is especially interesting and perfect, being hard, dark, and transparent, and affords the best opportunity that ever offers for examining the bottom where it is shallow; for you can lie at your length on ice only an inch thick, like a skater insect on the surface of the water, and study the bottom at your leisure, only two or three inches distant, like a picture behind a glass, and the water is necessarily always smooth then. There are many furrows in the sand where some creature has travelled about and doubled on its tracks; and for wrecks, it is strewn with the cases of cadis worms made of minute grains of white quartz.[35]

It's impossible for me not to picture Thoreau stretched out gingerly on the thin ice, careful to distribute the load of himself evenly so as not to punch through with his knee or the heel of his hand. His enormous blue-gray eyes are slightly crossed as he stares at the pond bottom two or three inches down, and his big hooked nose, touching the glazed surface, is starting to melt a little fairy birdbath in the ice. He shows you his body: "Look at my body as it is looking. This is what to do and how to do it, and this is what it's all about. Forget the cold; forget decorum; forget everything but looking—just your whole body looking." How did he get out there on the ice? He couldn't have just taken a couple of steps on it and lain down: the ice would have broken. He must have lain at the pond's margin and edged himself along little by little, sort of slithering—right arm, right leg, shoulder, hip—in a kind of squirmy swim. It's easy to see how the book infects the reader with picturing. Reading *Walden* with attention and engagement involves your whole body—a thorough reading requires the activity of all your cells.

Thoreau does not neglect the other senses. *Walden* has an entire section titled "Sounds." Here, for instance, are the whippoorwills:

Sometimes I heard four or five at once in different parts of the wood, by accident one a bar behind another, and so near me that I distinguished not only the cluck after each note, but

often that singular buzzing sound like a fly in a spider's web, only proportionally louder.[36]

Like many images in *Walden*, this one, a sound image, carries no rhetorical burden, has no persuading function, as the barn-pusher does. But the very preciseness of Thoreau's description and the active engagement of his imagination—"that singular buzzing sound like a fly in a spider's web"—honors these spots of sound and fills them with importance. This, I think, is the operation of the senses Thoreau has in mind when he praises "pure seeing" in the "Higher Laws" section. Pure seeing arises when all agenda are gone—only then can the senses operate in the presence of the spiritual imagination. Any of the senses can be involved. In *Walden*, sight happens to predominate, but Thoreau's whole body must have been zingingly alive. He loved to dance as well as sing, and at least once—when his family had a visitor, as it happens—he burst into dance, leaping over the parlor table. He loved, too, to wade deeply into the streams of the countryside wearing only his hat.

For Thoreau, the way to the lasting thing—reality, God, truth, the infinite—was through the exercise of the senses focused on the phenomena of the material world. Eternity was in the passing perception of fleeting things. The regeneration of the human soul was embodied in a ripple of water. Where is the insect now that seduced the snapping fish that rippled the water? Where is the fish? But we've got the ripple—well, sort of.

This kind of paradox is all over *Walden* and all over Thoreau: His contempt for possessions, for instance, and his fascination with the material world. His sensuousness and his spartan life. His spiritual nature and his full-bodied engagement with the world. Thoreau seems to have held all these things in a powerful, intuitive, and fluid resolution that he practiced to reimagine every day, all the time. It's something you can't hold down; you just have to leap over the table.

The impulse to represent *Walden* in pictures begins with Thoreau himself, who, in 1848, made a survey map of the pond. Walden Pond was, some claimed, bottomless, so one winter Thoreau drilled holes in the ice in a regular pattern and took soundings. He then made a rather beautiful scale drawing of the surface outline and the bottom of the pond—the drawing has an airy delicacy of line anchored by a pleasing graphic symmetry and decorated with little notes in his unreadable script.[37] It's a particularly appropriate first image, combining as it does technology and art and employing a physical representation to get at something that can't be seen—to access a mystery.

The version of this map printed in the first edition of *Walden* fails to convey the qualities of Thoreau's original. Similar characteristics are apparent, however, in the simple drawings of the natural world Thoreau began making in his journal in 1850. Some of these are reproduced in William Howarth's biography of Thoreau, *The Book of Concord*.[38]

One thing many of these journal sketches have in common with the Walden Pond map is their incorporation of the unseen. The most obvious examples are the drawings of animal tracks. This presence of the invisible is also indicated by Thoreau's economy of representation in his sketches of "migrating geese" and "scarlet oak leaf." Because the geese are just the weight of birds on the weight of air, just arc of flight and mounting air, we see (at least I see) the *air*.

Thoreau makes explicit this active relationship between the seen and the unseen in his discussion of the scarlet oak leaf. It is shaped by "what is not leaf and . . . what is leaf."[39] He refers to the leaf's outline as a coastline with "bays and headlands," implying the interaction of water and land. The very emptiness of the drawn image gives the leaf-space and the not-leaf-space similar status, space defined by line. Both spaces constitute a body of pressure bearing against an irregular, skinny border. The curve of the stem is just extra joy, flipped in space, for free.

Thoreau's drawings are a graphic counterpart to his ideas about pure seeing—the belief that if we look without an agenda, without "clutter," what is holy—the unadorned essence of a thing—will show through.

A drawing his sister Sophia made of his cabin on Walden Pond appeared in the first edition of *Walden*. In contrast to Thoreau's probing of the pond's depth, Sophia looks up the northern slope to his little peaked-roofed house perched among the trees. There's a striking difference between the spacious spareness of his drawing and the crowded-cozy romanticism of hers. Thoreau thought the slope of the roof in Sophia's drawing was inaccurate, too steep. What also seems inaccurate is the conventional sentiment the romanticism imposes on the representation. Compared with her brother's sketches, it is smothery and over-drawn; a sort of snuggly wildishness

takes up all the room.

There's no air, and no room for what cannot be seen.

Almost a hundred years after Thoreau lived at Walden Pond, *Thoreau's Walden: A Photographic Register*, Henry B. Kane's beautiful collection of black-and-white photographs of Walden Pond and the adjoining woods, was published.[40] By then, the site had become a state park. In his introduction to the book, Brooks Atkinson seems eager to convince his readers that the photographs represent the authentic Walden Pond, unaltered since Thoreau himself looked on it—the same scenes, skies, and animals. He also maintains that just out of camera view, Thoreau is still there: by capturing the very images Thoreau gazed on, we can recover Thoreau. Although this claim echoes Thoreau's gift for recognizing the invisible that inhabits what can be seen, it is wishful, conventional, and romantic thinking, in the same vein in which we kid ourselves that photographs will bring the past to us or us to the past. The link between the photographs and Walden Pond, like the link between picturing and *Walden*, is more legitimate. It lies in the variety of genius that is activated through images, the genius for seeing. Atkinson strikes a truer note when he writes that the photographer "had to have some of Thoreau's faith in the importance of what he was doing." He had to approach the scene as Thoreau did, "serve it patiently, study its properties, respond to its moods, believe in its holiness."[41]

The Walden Pond of today is not the Walden Pond of 1846. It's not even the Walden Pond of last week. How could it be? That's not to say that we're not glad it's there in its current incarnation or that it doesn't feel like a tangible, to some of us maybe an almost holy, link to the Philosophic Woodchuck—like your great-grandmother's wedding dress, which induces you, if you slip your hand inside, to nearly hallucinate the teenager who wore it. But I propose that a more intimate connection with the shaggy genius of Concord, and an action that honors him, consists in the practice of *seeing*, that central exercise of his genius. The photographs by Charles Gurche on the following pages, taken at many locations, picture not Walden Pond but *Walden*. Like the book, they are the fruit and record of episodes of alert and patient attention at a number of places and over a period of time. The combination of Thoreau's words and Gurche's photographs constitutes very good company and provides an occasion for flexing one's own genius and thereby connecting with what there is of Thoreau that is still available. This good company offers a possibility for waking up all over to a Thoreauvian quality of attention, to alert waiting, to the conviction that it matters.

Dona Budd

NOTES

1. Henry David Thoreau, *Journal*, B. Torrey. ed., vol. 1 in *The Writings of Henry David Thoreau* Walden edition (Boston: Houghton Mifflin, 1906), 380–81. The Walden edition has twenty volumes, fourteen of which are the *Journal*.

2. Carl Bode, ed., *The Portable Thoreau* (New York: Penguin, 1982), 441.

3. Ibid., 440.

4. Ibid., 542.

5. Ibid., 374–75.

6. Barzillia Frost, MS, (funeral sermon for John Thoreau Jr.) collection of George L. Davenport Jr. Quoted in Walter Harding, *The Days of Henry Thoreau* (New York: Knopf, 1965), 135.

7. James T. Fields, "Our Poet-Naturalist," *Baldwin's Monthly*, April 1877. Quoted in Harding, *Days of Henry Thoreau*, 20.

8. Bode, *Portable Thoreau*, 306.

9. Ibid., 343.

10. Mrs. Daniel Chester French, *Memories of a Sculptor's Wife* (Boston: n.p., 1928), 95. Quoted in Harding, *Days of Henry Thoreau*, 404.

11. MS, New York Public Library.

12. Henry David Thoreau, *Correspondence* (New York: New York University Press, 1958), 245–46. Quoted in Harding, *Days of Henry Thoreau*, 259–60.

13. Louisa May Alcott, "Merry's Monthly Chat with His Friends," *Merry's Museum*, March 1869. Quoted in Harding, *Days of Henry Thoreau*, 192.

14. Frederick L. H. Willis, *Alcott Memoirs* (Boston: n.p., 1915), 91–93. Quoted in Harding, *Days of Henry Thoreau*, 193.

15. James Kendall Hosmer, *The Last Leaf* (New York: n.p., 1912), 235–36. Quoted in Harding, *Days of Henry Thoreau*, 255.

16. Thoreau, *Journal*, vol. 1, 3.

17. Ibid., vol. 14, 346.

18. Bode, *Portable Thoreau*, 564–65.

19. Thoreau, *Journal*, vol. 5, 459.

20. Bode, *Portable Thoreau*, 324.

21. Thoreau, *Correspondence*, 245. Quoted in Harding, *Days of Henry Thoreau*, 259.

22. "Reminiscences of Thoreau," *Outlook* 63 (1899): 920. Quoted in Harding, *Days of Henry Thoreau*, 455.

23. Anna Ricketson and Walton Ricketson, *Daniel Ricketson and His Friends* (Boston: Houghton Mifflin, 1902), 135. Quoted in Harding, *Days of Henry Thoreau*, 456.

24. Ricketson and Ricketson, *Ricketson and His Friends*, 214. Quoted in Harding, *Days of Henry Thoreau*, 456–57.

25. Thoreau, *Correspondence*, 641. Quoted in Harding, *Days of Henry Thoreau*, 457.

26. Ricketson and Ricketson, *Ricketson and His Friends*, 136–37. Quoted in Harding, *Days of Henry Thoreau*, 460.

27. Harding, *Days of Henry Thoreau*, 460.

28. Ricketson and Ricketson, *Ricketson and His Friends*, 141–42. Quoted in Harding, *Days of Henry Thoreau*, 464.

29. Annie Russell Marble, *Thoreau: His Home, Friends, and Books* (New York: Cromwell, 1902), 180. Quoted in Harding, *Days of Henry Thoreau*, 466.

30. Bode, *Portable Thoreau*, 260–61.

31. Ibid., 363.

32. Ibid., 436–37.

33. Ibid., 525.

34. Ibid., 444.

35. Ibid., 490–91.

36. Ibid., 375–76.

37. A print of this drawing is available for viewing at the Bancroft Library at the University of California, Berkeley.

38. William Howarth, *The Book of Concord: Thoreau's Life as a Writer* (New York: Viking, 1982).

39. Henry David Thoreau, *Excursions* (Boston: Ticknor and Fields, 1863). Quoted in Howarth, *Book of Concord*, 171.

40. Henry B. Kane, *Thoreau's Walden: A Photographic Register* (New York: Knopf, 1946).

41. Ibid., viii.

The Photographs

by Charles Gurche

with excerpts from *Walden*

$\mathcal{I}$ went to the woods
because I wished to live
deliberately, to front only
the essential facts of life,
and see if I could not learn
what it had to teach, and not,
when I came to die, discover
that I had not lived.

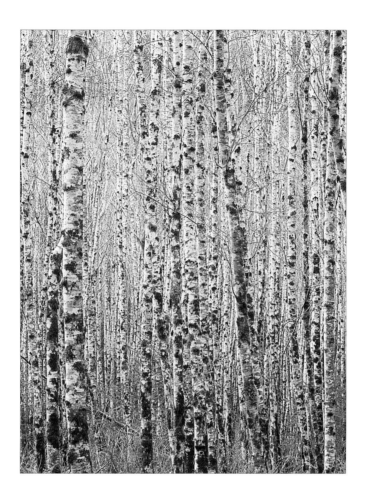

*F*or human society I was obliged to conjure up the former occupants of these woods. Within the memory of many of my townsmen the road near which my house stands resounded with the laugh and gossip of inhabitants, and the woods which border it were notched and dotted here and there with their little gardens and dwellings, though it was then much more shut in by the forest than now.

*O*ur village life would stagnate if it were not for the unexplored forests and meadows which surround it.

The earth is not a mere fragment of dead history, stratum upon stratum like the leaves of a book, to be studied by geologists and antiquaries chiefly, but living poetry like the leaves of a tree, which precede flowers and fruit —not a fossil earth, but a living earth.

I have never felt lonesome, or in the least oppressed by a sense of solitude, but once, and that was a few weeks after I came to the woods, when, for an hour, I doubted if the near neighborhood of man was not essential to a serene and healthy life. . . . But I was at the same time conscious of a slight insanity in my mood, and seemed to foresee my recovery. In the midst of a gentle rain while these thoughts prevailed, I was suddenly sensible of such sweet and beneficent society in Nature, in the very pattering of the drops, and in every sound and sight around my house, an infinite and unaccountable friendliness all at once like an atmosphere sustaining me, as made the fancied advantages of human neighborhood insignificant, and I have never thought of them since.

The indescribable innocence and beneficence of Nature—of sun and wind and rain, of summer and winter —such health, such cheer, they afford forever! and such sympathy have they ever with our race, that all Nature would be affected, and the sun's brightness fade, and the winds would sigh humanely, and the clouds rain tears, and the wood shed their leaves and put on mourning in midsummer, if any man should ever for a just cause grieve. Shall I not have intelligence with the earth? Am I not partly leaves and vegetable mould myself?

*I*nstead of calling on some scholar, I paid many a visit to particular trees, of kinds which are rare in this neighborhood, standing far away in the middle of some pasture, or in the depths of a wood or swamp, or on a hill-top. . . . These were the shrines I visited both summer and winter.

*T*he mass of men lead lives of quiet desperation. What is called resignation is confirmed desperation. From the desperate city you go into the desperate country, and have to console yourself with the bravery of minks and muskrats.

Nothing so fair, so pure, and at the same time so large, as a lake, perchance, lies on the surface of the earth. Sky water. It needs no fence. Nations come and go without defiling it. It is a mirror which no stone can crack, whose quicksilver will never wear off, whose gilding Nature continually repairs.

I did not wish to take a cabin passage, but rather to go before the mast and on the deck of the world, for there I could best see the moonlight amid the mountains.

The frost comes out of the ground like a dormant quadruped from its burrow, and seeks the sea with music, or migrates to other climes in clouds. Thaw with his gentle persuasion is more powerful than Thor with his hammer. The one melts, the other but breaks in pieces.

Many of the phenomena of Winter are suggestive of an inexpressible tenderness and fragile delicacy. We are accustomed to hear this king described as a rude and boisterous tyrant; but with the gentleness of a lover he adorns the tresses of Summer.

*T*his is the frost coming out of the ground; this is Spring. It precedes the green and flowery spring, as mythology precedes regular poetry. I know of nothing more purgative of winter fumes and indigestions. It convinces me that Earth is still in her swaddling clothes, and stretches forth baby fingers on every side.

They were pleasant spring days, in which the winter of man's discontent was thawing as well as the earth, and the life that had lain torpid began to stretch itself.

———————————•>———————————

In a pleasant spring morning
all men's sins are forgiven. Such a day
is a truce to vice.

$\mathcal{A}$s every seems
best to us in its turn, so the
coming in of spring is like
the creation of Cosmos out
of Chaos and the realization
of the Golden Age.

*B*y standing on tiptoe I could catch a glimpse of some of the peaks of the still bluer and more distant mountain ranges in the northwest, those true-blue coins from heaven's own mint.

I have penetrated to those meadows on the morning of many a first spring day, jumping from hummock to hummock, from willow root to willow root, when the wild river valley and the woods were bathed in so pure and bright a light as would have waked the dead, if they had been slumbering in their graves, as some suppose. There needs no stronger proof of immortality.

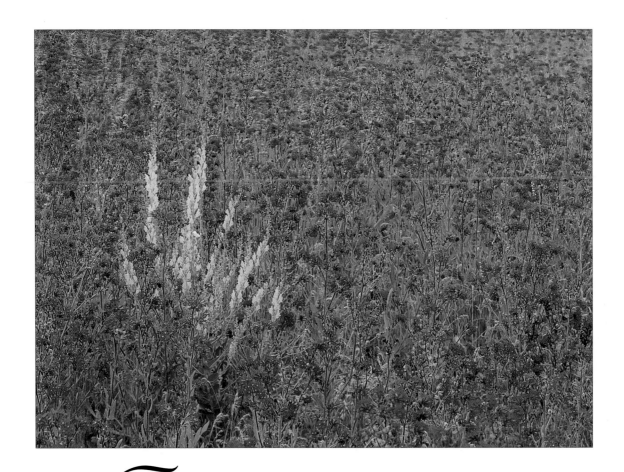

*T*here are no larger fields than these, no worthier games than may here be played. Grow wild according to thy nature, like these sedges and brakes, which will never become English hay.

---

*T*he grass flames up on the hillsides like a spring fire . . . as if the earth sent forth an inward heat to greet the returning sun; not yellow but green is the color of its flame —the symbol of perpetual youth, the grass-blade, like a long green ribbon, streams from the sod into the summer, checked indeed by the frost, but anon pushing on again, lifting its spear of last year's hay with the fresh life below.

Why should we be in such desperate haste to succeed, and in such desperate enterprises? If a man does not keep pace with his companions, perhaps it is because he hears a different drummer. Let him step to the music which he hears, however measured or far away. It is not important that he should mature as soon as an apple-tree or an oak. Shall he turn his spring into summer? If the condition of things which we were made for is not yet, what were any reality which we can substitute?

*W*hat is the pill which will keep us well, serene, contented?
Not my or thy great-grandfather's, but our great-grandmother
Nature's universal, vegetable, botanic medicines, by which
she has kept herself young always.

I am no more lonely than a single mullein or dandelion in a pasture, or a bean leaf, or sorrel, or a horsefly, or a humble-bee. I am no more lonely than the Mill Brook, or a weathercock, or the northstar, or the south wind, or an April shower, or a January thaw, or the first spider in a new house.

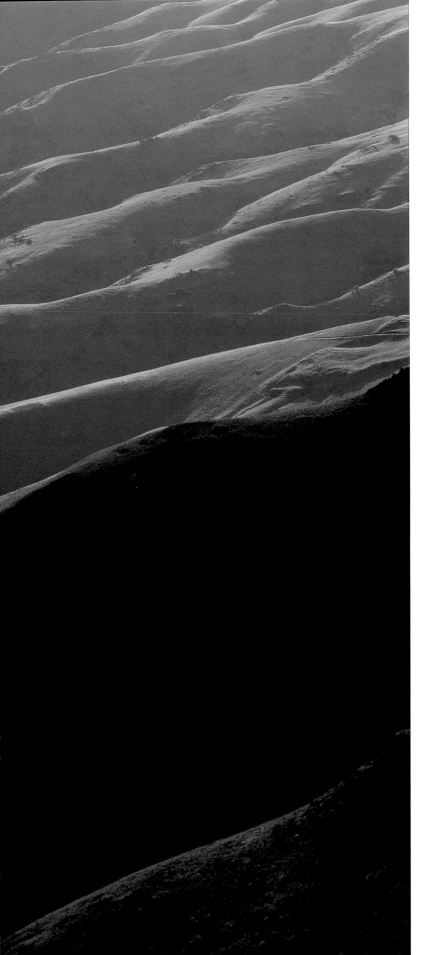

From a hill top near by, where the wood had been recently cut off, there was a pleasing vista southward across the pond, through a wide indentation in the hills which form the shore there, where their opposite sides sloping toward each other suggested a stream flowing out in that direction through a wooded valley, but stream there was none. That way I looked between and over the near green hills to some distant and higher ones in the horizon, tinged with blue.

$\mathcal{T}$he life in us is like the water in the river. It may rise this year
higher than man has ever known it, and flood the
parched uplands; even this may be the eventful year,
which will drown out all our muskrats.

*T*his small lake was of most value as a neighbor in the intervals of a gentle rain storm in August, when, both air and water being perfectly still, but the sky overcast, mid-afternoon had all the serenity of evening, and the wood-thrush sang around, and was heard from shore to shore. A lake like this is never smoother than at such a time; and the clear portion of the air above it being shallow and darkened by clouds, the water, full of light and reflections, becomes a lower heaven itself so much the more important.

*S*ee these clouds; how they hang!
That's the greatest thing I have seen to-day.

I should be glad if all the meadows on earth were left in a wild state, if that were the consequence of men's beginning to redeem themselves.

*W*e are wont to forget that the sun looks on our cultivated fields and on the prairies and forests without distinction. They all reflect and absorb his rays alike, and the former make but a small part of the glorious picture which he beholds in his daily course. In his view the earth is all equally cultivated like a garden.

$\mathcal{M}$any think that seeds improve with age. I have no doubt that time discriminates between the good and the bad; and when at last I shall plant, I shall be less likely to be disappointed. But I would say to my fellows, once for all, As long as possible live free and uncommitted. It makes but little difference whether you are committed to a farm or the county jail.

*I*f the day and the night are such that you greet them with joy, and life emits a fragrance like flowers and sweet-scented herbs, is more elastic, more starry, more immortal—that is your success.

*C*ultivate poverty like a garden herb, like sage. Do not trouble yourself much to get new things, whether clothes or friends. Turn the old; return to them. Things do not change; we change. Sell your clothes and keep your thoughts. God will see that you do not want society.

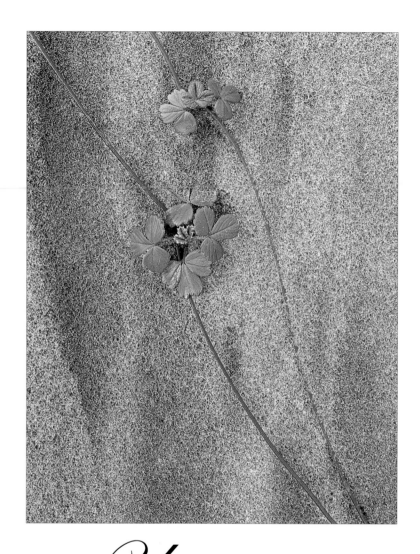

$\mathcal{Y}$ou may melt your metals
and cast them into the most
beautiful moulds you can; they will
never excite me like the forms
which this molten earth
flows out into.

*T*wonder what the world is doing now.
I have not heard so much as a locust over
the sweet-fern these three hours.

Let us spend one day as deliberately as Nature,
and not be thrown off the track by every nutshell
and mosquito's wing that falls on the rails.

It is well to have some water in your neighborhood, to give buoyancy to and float the earth. One value even of the smallest well is, that when you look into it you see that earth is not continent but insular. This is as important as that it keeps butter cool.

hat do we want most to dwell near to? Not to many men surely, the depot, the post-office, the bar-room, the meeting-house, the school-house, the grocery, Beacon Hill, or the Five Points, where men most congregate, but to the perennial source of our life, whence in all our experience we have found that to issue; as the willow stands near the water and sends out its roots in that direction.

$\mathscr{A}$lready, by the first of September, I had seen two or three small maples turned scarlet across the pond, beneath where the white stems of three aspens diverged, at the point of a promontory, next the water. Ah, many a tale their color told! And gradually from week to week the character of each tree came out, and it admired itself reflected in the smooth mirror of the lake.

𝒯he forest has never so good a setting, nor is so distinctly beautiful, as when seen from the middle of a small lake amid hills which rise from the water's edge; for the water in which it is reflected not only makes the best foreground in such a case, but, with its winding shore, the most natural and agreeable boundary to it.

Whenever I looked out
on the pond it impressed me
like a tarn high up on the side
of a mountain, its bottom far
above the surface of other lakes,
and, as the sun arose, I saw it
throwing off its nightly clothing
of mist, and here and there,
by degrees, its soft ripples or
its smooth reflecting surface
was revealed.

The cart before the horse is neither beautiful nor useful. Before we can adorn our houses with beautiful objects the walls must be stripped, and our lives must be stripped, and beautiful housekeeping and beautiful living be laid for a foundation: now, a taste for the beautiful is most cultivated out of doors, where there is no house and no housekeeper.

While I enjoy the friendship of the seasons I trust that nothing can make life a burden to me.

*L*ike the wasps, before I finally went into winter quarters in November, I used to resort to the north-east side of Walden, which the sun, reflected from the pitch-pine woods and the stony shore, made the fire-side of the pond; it is so much pleasanter and wholesomer to be warmed by the sun while you can be, than by an artificial fire. I thus warmed myself by the still glowing embers which the summer, like a departed hunter, had left.

*O*nly that day dawns to which we are awake. There is more day to dawn. The sun is but a morning star.

*A*ll poets and heroes, like Memnon, are the children of Aurora, and emit their music at sunrise. To him whose elastic and vigorous thought keeps pace with the sun, the day is a perpetual morning. It matters not what the clocks say or the attitudes and labors of men. Morning is when I am awake and there is a dawn in me.

*T*here can be no very black melancholy to him
who lives in the midst of Nature and has his sense
still. There was never yet such a storm but it was
Aeolian music to a healthy and innocent ear.

*I*n any weather, at any hour of the day or night, I have been anxious to improve the nick of time, and notch it on my stick too; to stand on the meeting of two eternities, the past and future, which is precisely the present moment; to toe that line.

*T*he winds which passed over my dwelling were such as sweep over the ridges of mountains, bearing the broken strains, or celestial parts only, of terrestrial music. The morning wind forever blows, the poem of creation is uninterrupted; but few are the ears that hear it. Olympus is but the outside of the earth every where.

*B*ut no weather interfered fatally with my walks, or rather my going abroad, for I frequently tramped eight or ten miles through the deepest snow to keep an appointment with a beech-tree, or a yellow-birch, or an old acquaintance among the pines; when the ice and snow causing their limbs to droop, and so sharpening their tops, had changed the pines into fir-trees.

$\mathcal{T}$his is a delicious evening, when the whole body is one sense, and imbibes delight through every pore. I go and come with a strange liberty in Nature, a part of herself.

FURTHER READING

Bode, Carl, ed. *Collected Poems of Henry Thoreau.* Enl. ed. Baltimore: Johns Hopkins University Press, 1970.

_____. *The Portable Thoreau.* Riverside ed. New York: Penguin, 1982. This edition contains an unabridged version of *Walden* and a wide selection from Thoreau's other works, including *A Week on the Concord and Merrimack Rivers,* "Civil Disobedience," journal entries, poems, and more. Because it is more widely available than the Norton edition, page numbers in this book refer to the Riverside (Penguin) edition.

Harding, Walter. *The Days of Henry Thoreau.* New York: Knopf, 1965. The first comprehensive reliable biography of Thoreau, this is a very readable book.

Howarth, William. *The Book of Concord: Thoreau's Life as a Writer.* New York: Viking, 1982. This book contains some of Thoreau's botanical, wildlife, and landscape drawings.

Meyerson, Joel, ed. *The Cambridge Companion to Henry David Thoreau.* Cambridge: Cambridge University Press, 1995.

Milder, Robert. *Reimagining Thoreau.* Cambridge: Cambridge University Press, 1995. This very useful and interesting revised conception of Thoreau is a more challenging biography that takes into account developing scholorship and ideas.

Thoreau, Henry David. *Walden.* New York: Norton, 1992. In addition to *Walden,* this Norton edition contains *Resistance to Civil Government,* selections from Thoreau's journal, contemporary book reviews, and critical essays.

Westbrook, Perry D. *A Literary History of New England.* Bethlehem, Pa.: Lehigh University Press, 1988.

SELECTED WORKS BY HENRY DAVID THOREAU

BOOKS

Cape Cod. With introduction by Paul Theroux. New York: Penguin, 1987.

Journal. Edited by John C. Broderick et al. Princeton: Princeton University Press, 1981–1992.

Letters to Various Persons, Darby, Pa.: Folcroft Library Edition, 1971.

The Maine Woods. Edited by Joseph J. Moldenhauer. Princeton: Princeton University Press, 1972.

A Week on the Concord and Merrimack Rivers. Edited by Carl Hovde and Textual Center Staff, William L. Howarth, Elizabeth Witherell. Princeton: Princeton University Press, 1980.

Yankee in Canada. Montreal: Harvest House, 1961.

ESSAYS

"Civil Disobedience"

"The Last Days of John Brown"

"Life without Principle"

"The Natural History of Massachusetts"

"Slavery in Massachusetts"

"The Succession of Forest Trees"

"Walking, or the Wild"

Note: The various collections of Thoreau's works each contain some, but not all, of these essays. All of the essays in this list, except the last two, appear in the Riverside (Penguin) edition of *The Portable Thoreau.* At the time of this writing, Princeton University Press is in the process of producing the complete works. When its edition of the essays appears, it will be the best— and the only complete—source.